NATHAN LANE
A FUNNY THING HAPPENED ON THE WAY TO THE
FORUM

CONTENTS

Photography: Joan Marcus

Applications for performance of this work, whether legitimate, stock,
amateur, or foreign, should be addressed to:
MUSIC THEATRE INTERNATIONAL
545 Eighth Avenue
New York, NY 10018

EXCLUSIVELY DISTRIBUTED BY

7777 W. BLUEMOUND RD. P.O. BOX 13819 MILWAUKEE, WI 53213

Nathan Lane and Leigh Zimmmerman

Nathan Lane, Mark Linn-Baker, Ernie Sabella and Lewis J. Stadlen

Nathan Lane

The Company

Comedy Tonight

Words and Music by
STEPHEN SONDHEIM

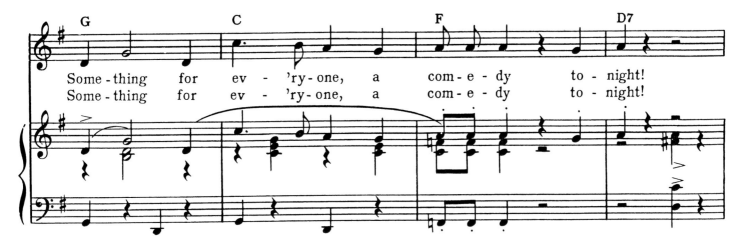

Some - thing for ev - 'ry - one, a com - e - dy to - night!
Some - thing for ev - 'ry - one, a com - e - dy to - night!

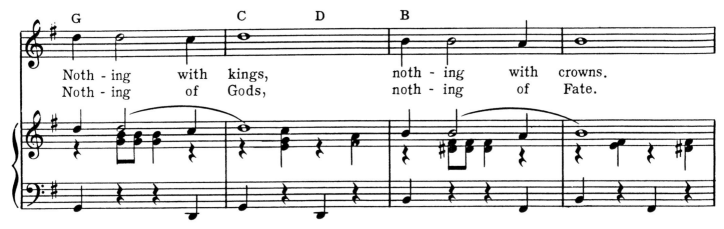

Noth - ing with kings, noth - ing with crowns.
Noth - ing of Gods, noth - ing of Fate.

Bring on the lov - ers, li - ars and clowns!__
Weigh - ty af - fairs will just have to wait.__

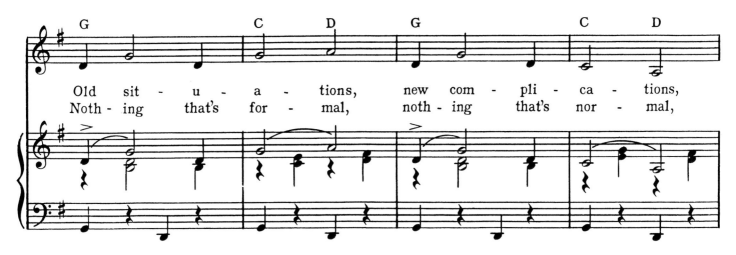

Old sit - u - a - tions, new com - pli - ca - tions,
Noth - ing that's for - mal, noth - ing that's nor - mal,

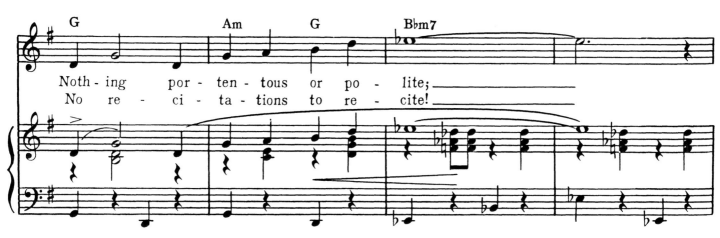

Noth - ing por - ten - tous or po - lite; ____
No re - ci - ta - tions to re - cite! ____

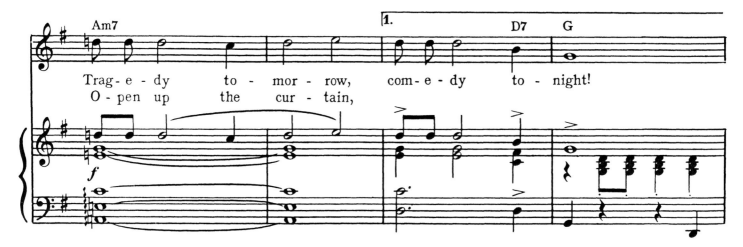

Trag - e - dy to - mor - row, com - e - dy to - night!
O - pen up the cur - tain,

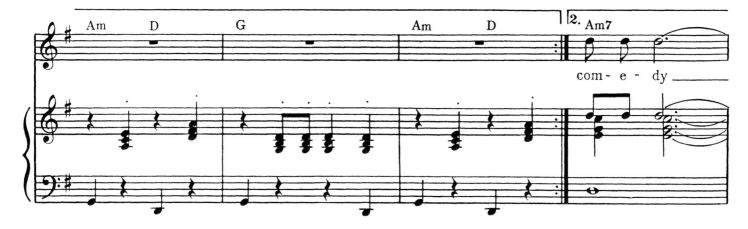

com - e - dy ____

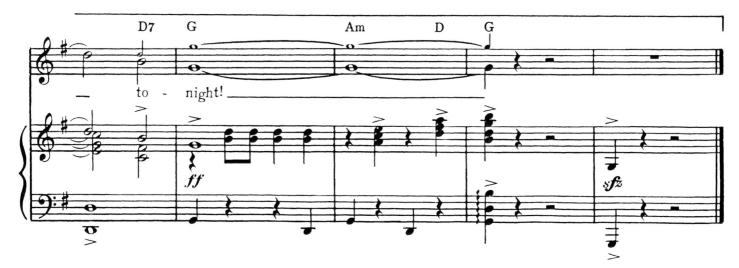

____ to - night! ____
____ to - night!

Impossible

Words and Music by
STEPHEN SONDHEIM

Refrain - With a lilt

Love, I Hear

Words and Music by
STEPHEN SONDHEIM

*Chord names represent only a simplified version of the harmonies.

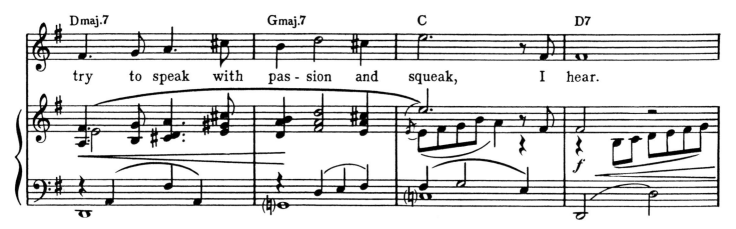

try to speak with pas-sion and squeak, I hear.

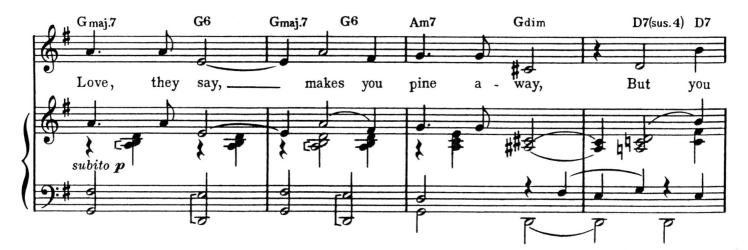

Love, they say, _____ makes you pine a - way, But you

pine a - way _____ with an id - i - ot - ic grin. _____ I'm

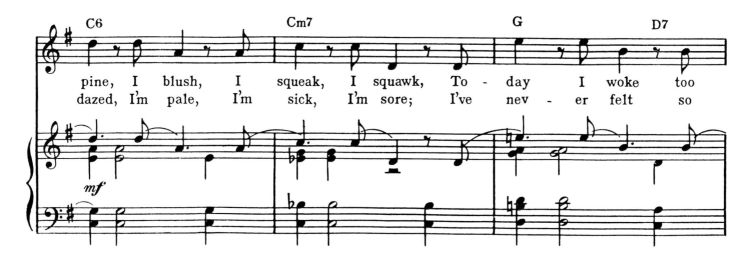

pine, I blush, I squeak, I squawk, To - day I woke too
dazed, I'm pale, I'm sick, I'm sore; I've nev - er felt so

weak   to walk.   What's   love,   I hear,   I   feel   I fear   I'm
well   be - fore!   What's   love,   I hear,   I   feel   I fear...   I

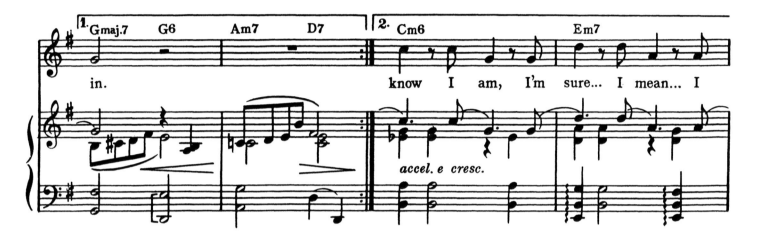

in.   know   I am,   I'm   sure...   I mean...   I

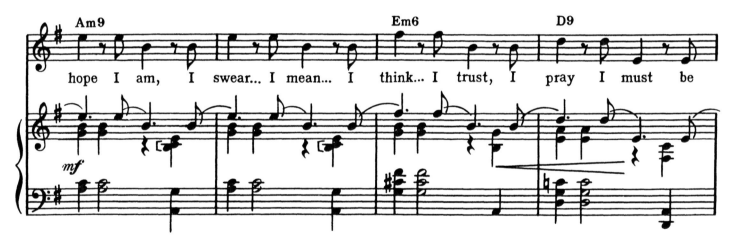

hope   I am,   I   swear...   I mean...   I   think...   I   trust,   I   pray   I must   be

in!

LOVELY

Words and Music by
STEPHEN SONDHEIM

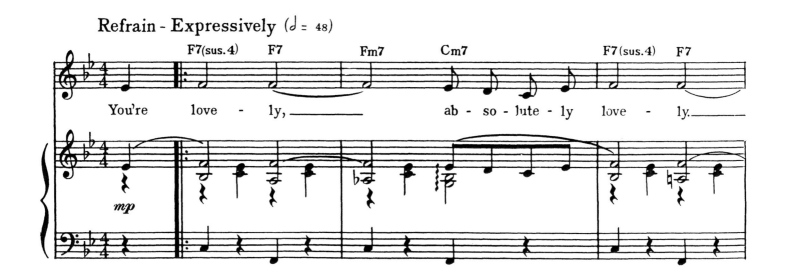

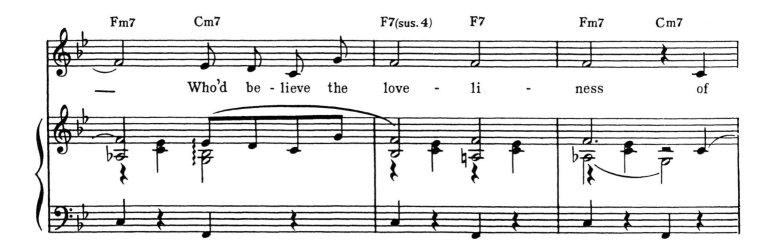

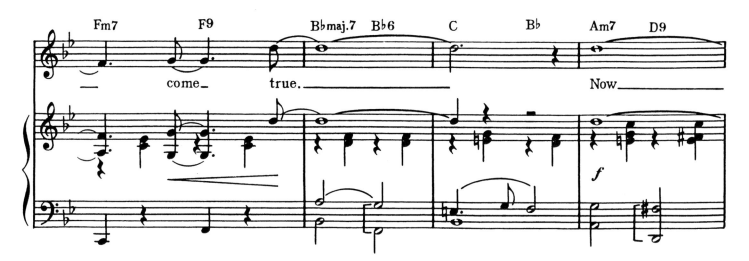

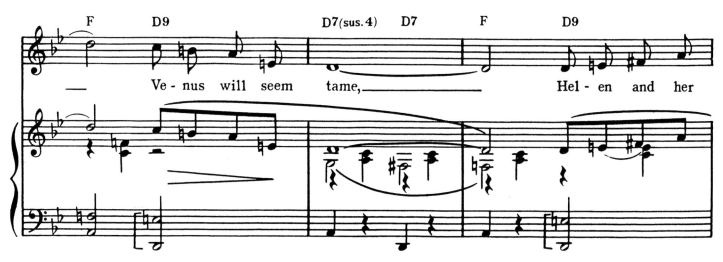

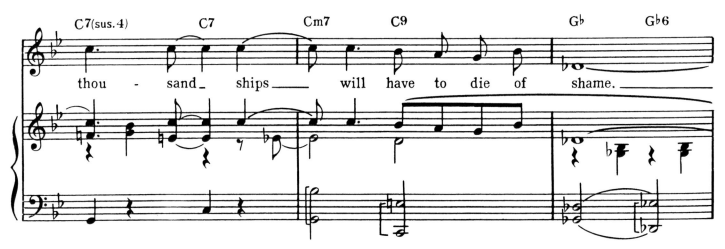

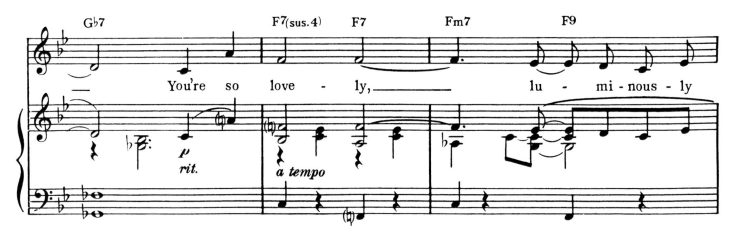

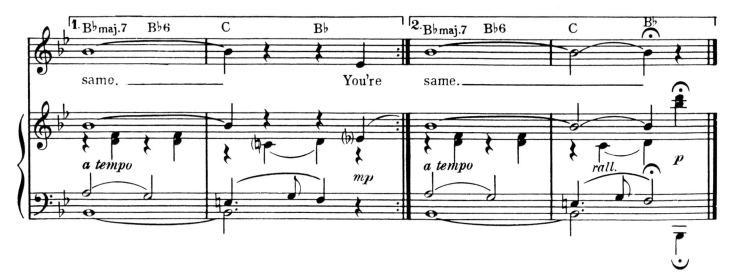

Pretty Little Picture

Words and Music by
STEPHEN SONDHEIM

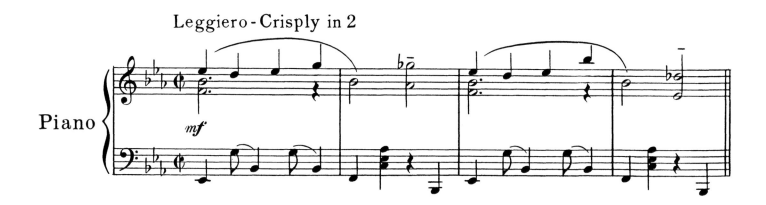

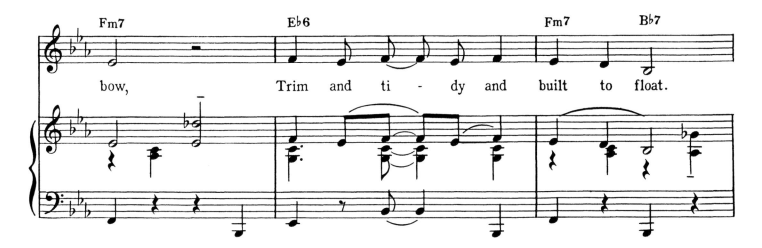

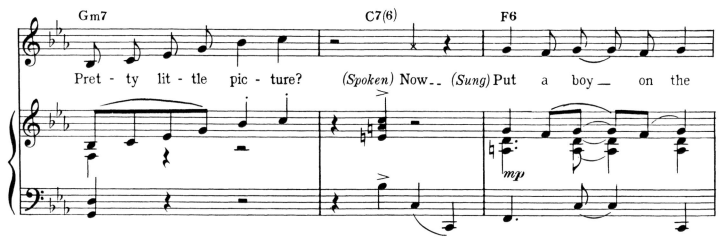

Pret - ty lit - tle pic - ture? *(Spoken)* Now__ *(Sung)* Put a boy__ on the

star - board side, Lean - ing out__ at the rail.

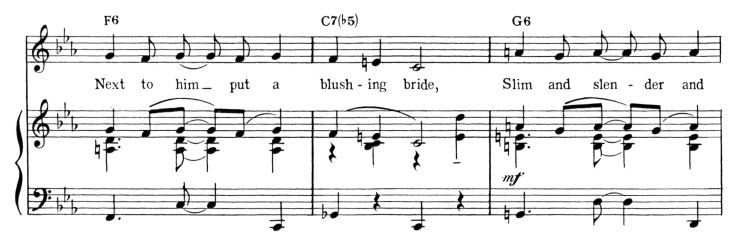

Next to him__ put a blush - ing bride, Slim and slen - der and

star - ry eyed. Down be - low__ put a ti - ny bed. The

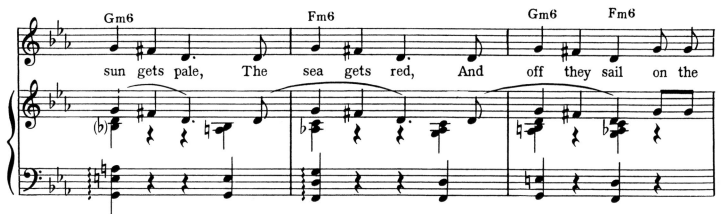

sun gets pale, The sea gets red, And off they sail on the

first high tide, The boat and the bed and the boy and the bride! It's a

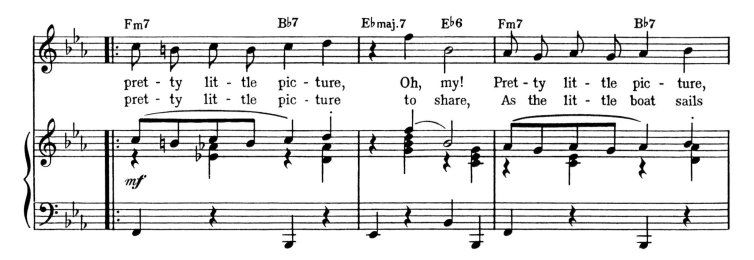

pret - ty lit - tle pic - ture, Oh, my! Pret - ty lit - tle pic - ture,
pret - ty lit - tle pic - ture to share, As the lit - tle boat sails

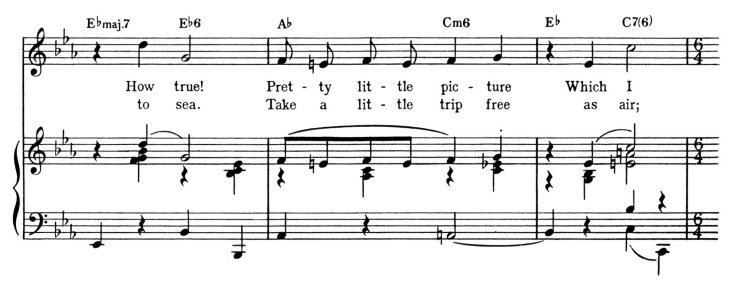

How true! Pret - ty lit - tle pic - ture Which I
to sea. Take a lit - tle trip free as air;

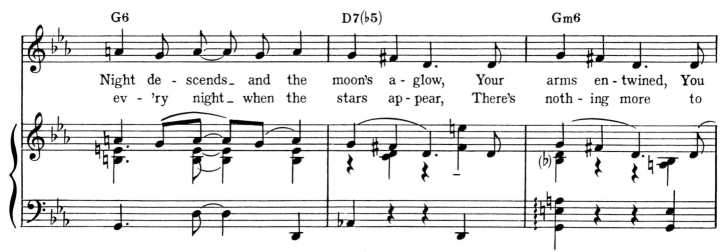

steal be - low, And far be - hind at the edge of day The
see or hear, There's just the shore where the lov - ers lie, The

bong of the bell of the bu - oy in the bay, And the
sand and the sea and the stars and the sky, And the

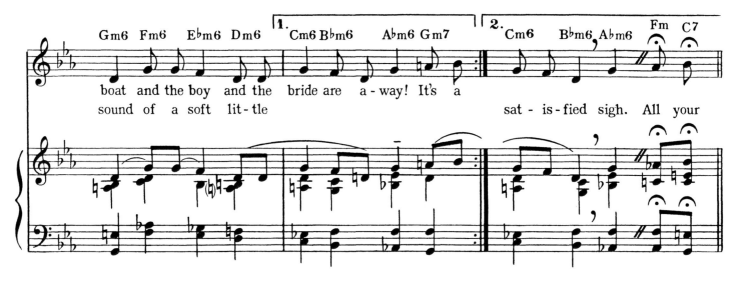

boat and the boy and the bride are a - way! It's a
sound of a soft lit - tle

sat - is - fied sigh. All your

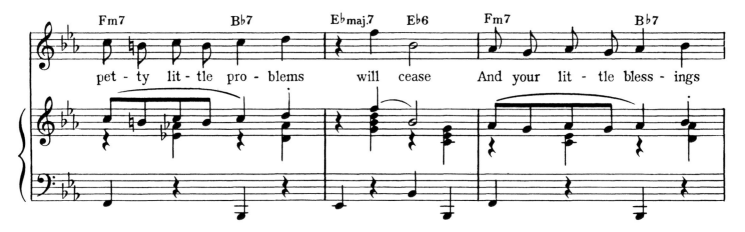

pet - ty lit - tle pro - blems will cease And your lit - tle bless - ings

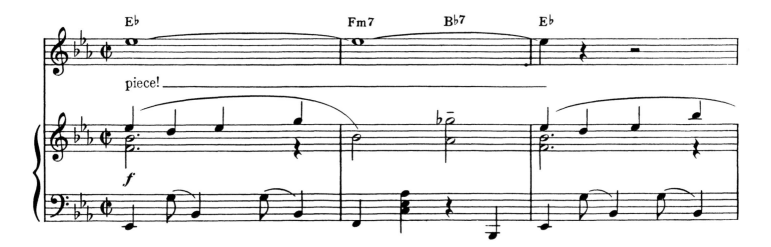

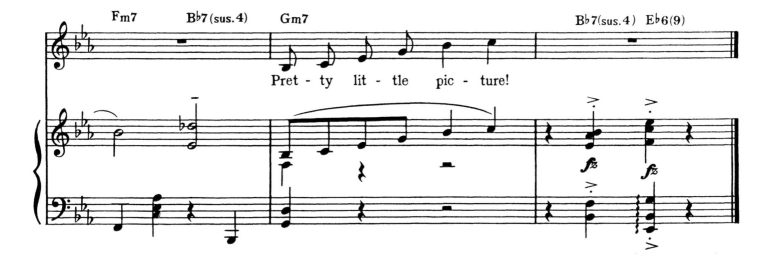

That'll Show Him

Words and Music by
STEPHEN SONDHEIM

you. So I'll hold him ten times as tight... That-'ll show him,

too! 1.When we're on his
2. I shall coo and

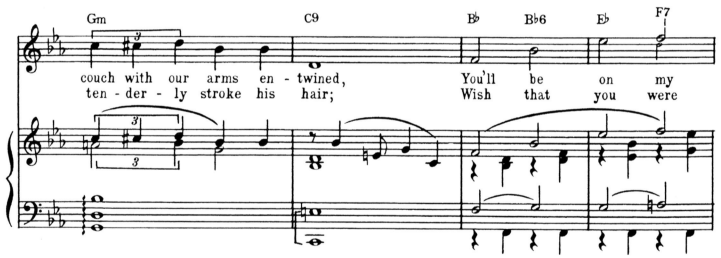

couch with our arms en-twined, You'll be on my
ten-der-ly stroke his hair; Wish that you were

mind. He'll be sor-ry! When it's eve-ning And we're in our
there. You'd en-joy it! For it real-ly will be you to

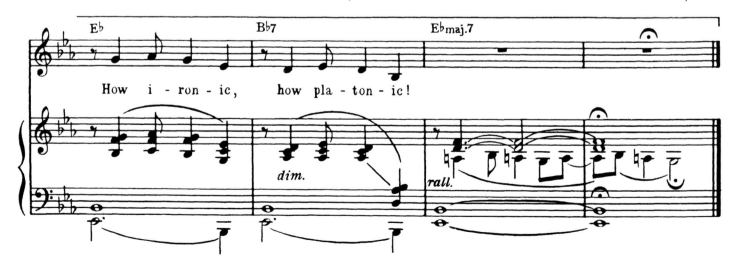

Everybody Ought To Have A Maid

Words and Music by
STEPHEN SONDHEIM

Flut-ter-ing up the stair - way, Shut-ter - ing up the win - dows,
Skit-ter-ing down the hall - way, Flit - ter - ing thru the par - lor,
(Alternate) { Pat-ter-ing thru the at - tic, Chat-ter - ing in the cel - lar,
Wrig-gl-ing in the an - te-room, Gig - gl - ing in the liv-ing-room,

Clut-ter-ing up the bed - room, But-ter-ing up the mas - ter, Put-ter-ing all a -
Tit-ter-ing in the pan - try, Lit-ter-ing up the bed - room,
Clat-ter-ing in the kit - chen, Flat-ter-ing in the bed - room,
Jig - gl-ing in the din-ing room, Wig-gl-ing in the oth - er rooms,

round the house! Put-ter - ing all a - round

the house!